The Internet

Meg Greve

rourkeeducationalmedia.com

Scan for Related Titles and Teacher Resources

Teaching Focus:

Text feature: Diagrams- How do the diagrams help you understand the information in the text?

Before Reading:

Building Academic Vocabulary and Background Knowledge

Before reading a book, it is important to set the stage for your child or student by using pre-reading strategies. This will help them develop their vocabulary, increase their reading comprehension, and make connections across the curriculum.

1. *Read the title and look at the cover. Let's make predictions about what this book will be about.*
2. *Take a picture walk by talking about the pictures/photographs in the book. Implant the vocabulary as you take the picture walk. Be sure to talk about the text features such as headings, Table of Contents, glossary, bolded words, captions, charts/ diagrams, or Index.*
3. Have students read the first page of text with you then have students read the remaining text.
4. *Strategy Talk – use to assist students while reading.*
   - *Get your mouth ready*
   - *Look at the picture*
   - *Think…does it make sense*
   - *Think…does it look right*
   - *Think…does it sound right*
   - *Chunk it – by looking for a part you know*
5. *Read it again.*
6. *After reading the book complete the activities below.*

Content Area Vocabulary
Use glossary words in a sentence.

device
network
online
packets
protocols
server

After Reading:

Comprehension and Extension Activity

After reading the book, work on the following questions with your child or students in order to check their level of reading comprehension and content mastery.

1. *What is the Internet? (Summarize)*
2. *What do you search for on the Internet? (Text to self connection)*
3. *What are some ways you can stay safe on the Internet? (Text to self connection)*
4. *How are the Internet and the World Wide Web different? (Asking questions)*

Extension Activity

Let's take a closer look at the World Wide Web. Open a browser and type in a search for something you are interested in, like cars, soccer, or a certain toy. How long did it take the World Wide Web to give you results? Were the results what you were looking for? For example, if you searched for cars did websites selling cars come up? Or, did websites for the Disney movie *Cars* appear? You need to be specific when searching. Try to search again but be a little more specific. For example, if you wanted to look up a particular soccer star you would type in that person's name. How are the results different this time?

Table of Contents

Information in a Flash!

Millions of people use the Internet to send and receive information every day. The best part is it all happens in a flash!

The World Wide Web went online in 1992.

Internet Abbreviation	Stands For . . .
www	World Wide Web
URL	Uniform Resource Locator
IP	Internet Protocol
ISP	Internet Service Provider
DNS	Domain Name System
HTTP	Hypertext Transfer Protocol

The Internet is not in your computer.

The Internet is a **network** of servers, or powerful computers.

Servers can speak many different languages. One of those is HTTP. This language allows your computer to explore the Web.

The Smaller Parts

The Internet has two main parts. The first part is the hardware. This includes anything that makes your computer work and connect to the Internet.

Hardware

smartphone

desktop computer

laptop computer

cell phone

electronic tablet

Protocols are the other big part of the Internet. The protocols are common rules that all computers follow so that information can be requested and sent.

How Does It Get There?

The Internet is connected in a similar way to how roads and streets connect a community. So every **device** in a network has its own address.

A computer's address is its IP address.

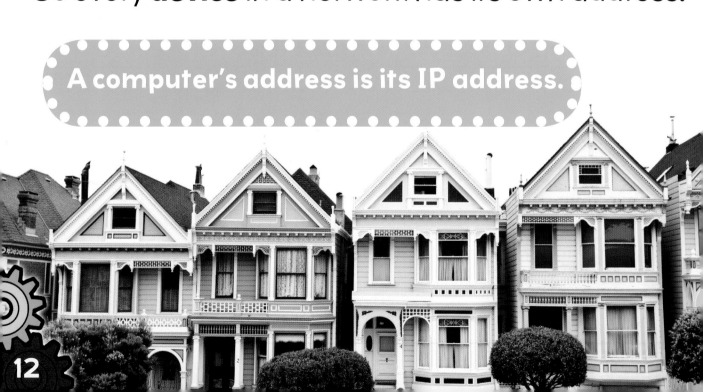

All websites have an IP address and URL starting with www.

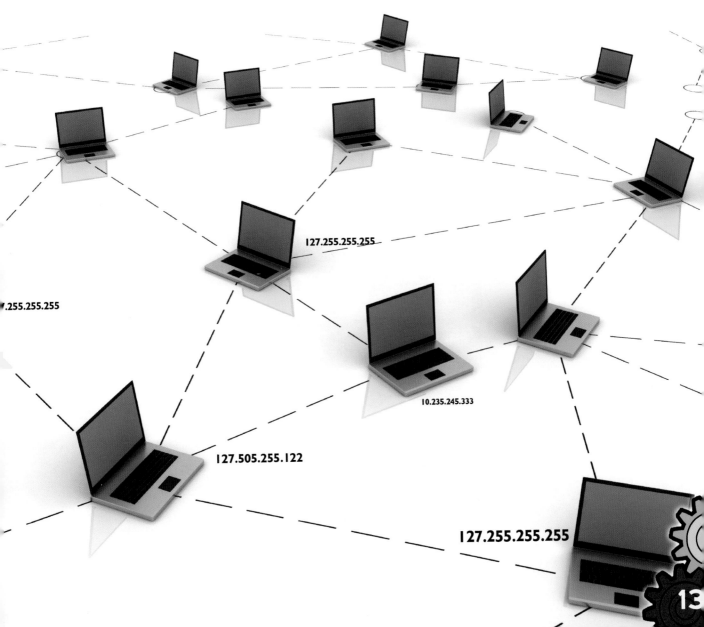

127.255.255.255

.255.255.255

10.235.245.333

127.505.255.122

127.255.255.255

13

Servers store the information we need. They may sell a product, play videos, or give you information about animals.

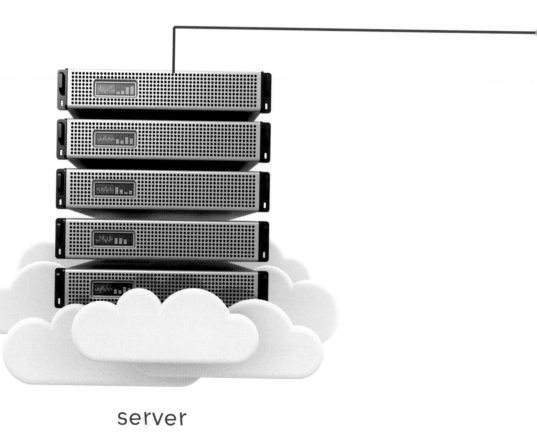

server

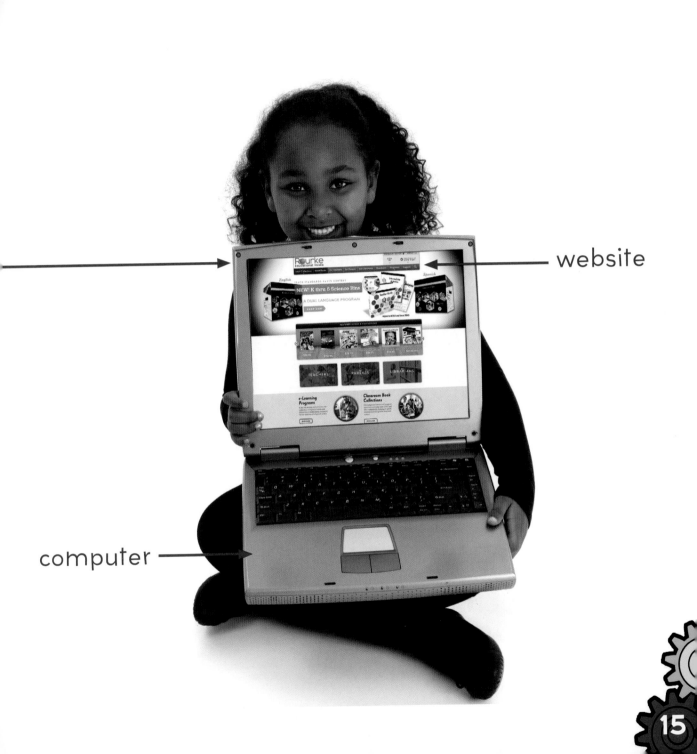

website

computer

Let's put all of these pieces together to see how the Internet works.

– First, you type in an URL.

– This is sent through your ISP, the company that connects you to the Internet.

– Your computer looks up a website's address in a DNS. It is like a big phone book for the Internet.

– A network of computers finds the **server** you want and sends back the information.

– It all happens in under a second!

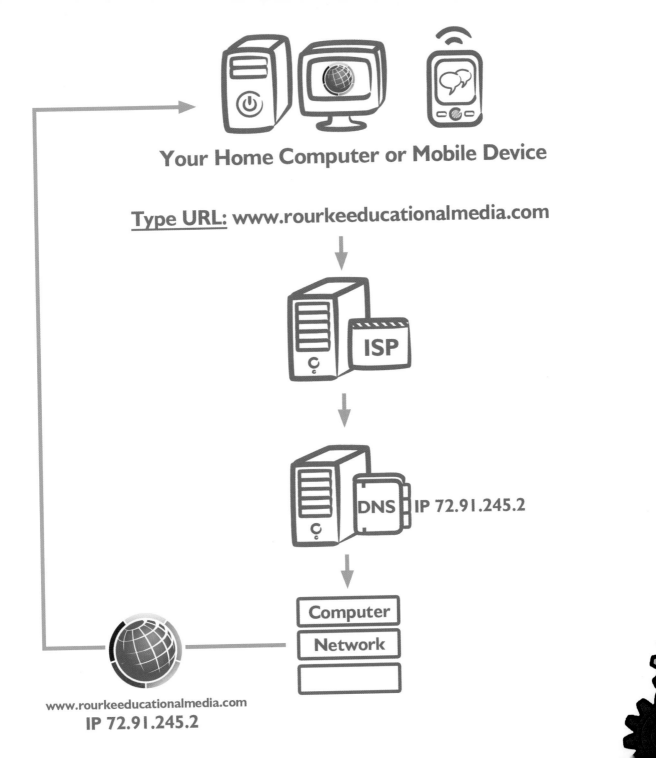

Your Home Computer or Mobile Device

Type URL: www.rourkeeducationalmedia.com

ISP

DNS IP 72.91.245.2

Computer

Network

www.rourkeeducationalmedia.com
IP 72.91.245.2

The information sent back does not come in one piece, but in **packets**. Your device puts the packets together so you can understand them.

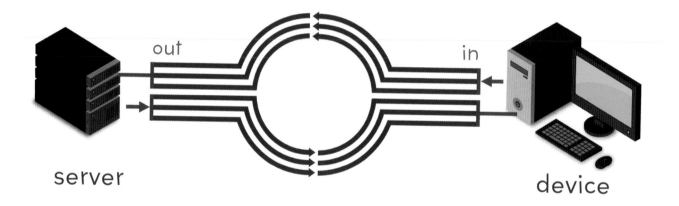

out

in

server

device

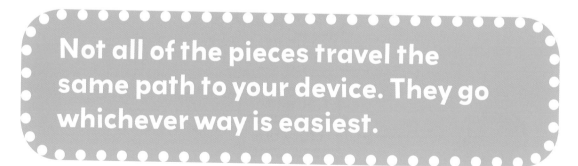

Not all of the pieces travel the same path to your device. They go whichever way is easiest.

What Is the Difference?

The Web is a way to share information **online**, but it is not the only piece of the Internet. Email and other data travel across the Internet as well.

Thanks to the Internet, information travels faster than ever before. People are working to make it faster and better every day.

The Internet has connected people all over the world.

Safety First!

Follow these safety tips to make the most of your time spent online.

1. Only open and send emails to people you know. Never open emails from people you do not know.
2. Make sure an adult knows when you are online. Find out which websites are okay for you to visit.
3. Never share personal information with anyone online.
4. Ask an adult before downloading something from the Internet. You could end up downloading something that will break your computer.
5. Remember, not everything you read on the Internet is true. Check information by reading it from a reliable source.

Photo Glossary

device (di-VISE): A computer or other electronic machine used to connect to the Internet.

network (NET-wurk): A group of things that are connected.

online (AWN-LINE): Connected to the Internet.

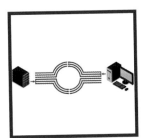 **packets** (PAK-its): Small pieces of a complete piece of information that is sent over the Internet.

 **protocols** (PROH-tuh-kawls): A set of rules about how data is moved between computers or over a network.

 **server** (SUR-vur): A computer shared by multiple users in a network.

Index

Websites to Visit

thekidshouldseethis.com/post/26674356049
www.kidzui.com
www.brainpop.com

About the Author

Meg Greve lives in Chicago with her husband Tom, and her two children, Madison and William. Meg uses the Internet to research, write, and share information about her books!

Meet The Author!
www.meetREMauthors.com

www.rourkeeducationalmedia.com

PHOTO CREDITS: Title Page, page 10 © Monkey Business Images; page 4 © PacoRomero Sirgunnik; page 5 © Vikram Raghuvanshi; page 6 © alexsl; page 8 © Anatolii Babii; page 9 © Bobboz; page 11 © Digital Photo Professional; page 12 © Adam Korzekwa; page 15 © PhotoEuphoria; page 19 © Paul Fleet; page 20 © Wavebreak Media Ltd

Edited by: Jill Sherman

Cover and Interior design by: Jen Thomas

Library of Congress PCN Data

The Internet/ Meg Greve
(How It Works)
ISBN (hard cover)(alk. paper) 978-1-62717-643-9
ISBN (soft cover) 978-1-62717-765-8
ISBN (e-Book) 978-1-62717-885-3
Library of Congress Control Number: 2014934211

Printed in the United States of America, North Mankato, Minnesota

Also Available as: